WHITE SUSTENANCE

Wick Poetry Chapbook Series
Maggie Anderson, Editor

Sleepwalking with Mayakovsky
Robert Brown

White Sustenance
Kat Snider Blackbird

WHITE SUSTENANCE

Kat Snider Blackbird

The Kent State University Press

Kent, Ohio, & London England

© 1994 by Kat Snider Blackbird
All Rights Reserved
Library of Congress Catalog Card Number 93-35959
ISBN 0-87338-503-9
Manufactured in the United States of America

The Wick Poetry Chapbook series is sponsored by the
Stan and Tom Wick Poetry Program and the Department
of English at Kent State University.

Library of Congress Cataloging-in-Publication Data
Blackbird, Kat Snider, 1955–
    White sustenance/Kat Snider Blackbird.
      p.   cm. — (Wick poetry chapbook series)
    ISBN 0-87338-503-9 (pbk.: alk.) ∞
    I. Title. II. Series.
PS3552.L34137W47 1994
811'. 54—dc20   93-35959
                                              CIP

British Library Cataloging-in-Publication data are available.

Despair's advantage is achieved
By suffering—Despair—
To be assisted of Reverse
One must Reverse have bore—

The Worthiness of Suffering like
The Worthiness of Death
Is ascertained by tasting—

As can no other Mouth

Of Savors—make us conscious—
As did ourselves partake—
Affliction feels impalpable
Until Ourselves are struck—

—Emily Dickinson, 799 (1863)

CONTENTS

ACKNOWLEDGMENTS

Grateful acknowledgment is made to the editors of the following publications in which these poems first appeared: "Writing Poems," *The New York Quarterly* 48 (1992); "The Great Blue Heron," *The Midwest Quarterly* (Summer 1993); "How to Get a Man," *Slipstream* 13 (Fall 1993); "Women You Have Loved," *The Lakeland Forum* (Fall 1992).

WOMEN YOU HAVE LOVED

So new to this old story,
I've asked you the names
of women you have loved.
I want to turn to the last page,
see how this pretty tale will end.
I read the names you speak
like words on tombstones
in an old cemetery,
lilacs purpling the dusky sky.

There is a certain comfort
walking here with these women.
I feel their hands
dimly moving over your body.
I hear their soft moaning,
their loneliness,
their long hair rustling the new leaves,
their breath whispering soft *oh's*
through hundred-year-old trees.

Only when you take my hand
am I afraid of death.
Only when I touch your skin,
cool and smooth as these granite markers,
do I hear their bones begin to rattle,
and far-off thunder drumming the sky,
closer, louder.

Only when you hold my face in your hands
do I hear my own beating heart.
And when you tuck me in
between the grass and your heaviness,
I move my fingers carefully over you,
searching again for the lines of their names
to tell me stories about death,
about what there is to fear,
and what not to fear.

CAVE DRAWINGS

Adjusting the eye to darkness
you enter slowly
carrying your transformation
juice   stain   dye

the colors you have captured
the blood of the hunt   the kill
the dance   the chant   the dream.

These are elusive substances.
In sun, they fade quickly,
turn to dust, and disappear.
But you are faithful to complete darkness.

Pushing farther into the heart,
you are the fugitive stag.
You will paint yourself.
You are herdsman of the wild
with beautiful antlers.

AT RISK

After making love on the floor
in front of the first fire
in my fireplace in over two years,
after looking at your face
in mostly moon, each sculpted bone,
and living for hours in the hollows
of your inner arms,
pools at your breast bone,
shoulder bones, shelter of hip bones,
bones of your jaw and your skull
and your exquisite fingers,
I am at risk.

Although the light has burned out
at the bottom of the basement stairs,
I go down anyway, feeling my way along
the painted wooden rail,
the grainy iron drainpipe,
the cold-edged basin.
I need to get to the washing machine
so my daughters will have socks
and underwear in the morning.
My belly pressed to white enamel
soaks in the vibrations of the spin cycle.
You will be leaving in the morning
and I will have laundry to fold.
I'm thinking, *What a shame
there is nothing anywhere in this house
shaped quite like your cock.*

I'm in love with you,
the billion lovers tell their
billion beloveds.
It is because you bent over me
and made your long hair dance across my skin,
a shiver, wind over water,
one says to hers. Another says,
It is because we told stories,
little boats on still ponds
in the mountains of Vermont;
a woman who keeps a lantern burning
for the road-weary traveler
in her thatch-roofed cottage
at the edge of an English moor.
It is because you said,
"Wait a minute," and we waited,
and then went again. Because you
held my knees tight to my shoulders.
Because you said the word
"beautiful."
That is what they say, the lovers.

There is an old black rocking chair
in my basement, and I'm sitting here
waiting through the rinse.
Some people add fabric softener about now
but I think it's a waste of money.
How soft can soft be?
I love you
because you opened the door for me,
because you carried the ashes
from my fireplace
down into my night-black backyard
and spread them gently,
as if they were my own,
into the turned earth
of my grave-shaped garden.

PETTY ADDICTIONS

At 2 A.M. you call me up
to tell me you need my help
as you enter this period of healing.
You've smoked five cigarettes tonight
at the Food Benefit where you probably
"overate."

I am addicted to love,
and I love you. All I can offer
is my silence and my empty hands.
And only occasionally am I quiet,
most often my hands think
they're people in a crowded room,
thickly socializing.

The little intervals of silence,
the rare instance my hands are empty,
are the crusts of moldy bread
the prison guard brings
every seventh day. My eyes
blacken with hunger.

My hunger is making me crazy,
making me do crazy things,
like devour this gray bread
without a thought of your sunken eyes.
Before I have swallowed,
I'm wracked with the thought
of stealing what little
the guard is bringing you.

HOW TO GET A MAN

You have heard many sermons
and have carried
your own interpretations
locked in your heart
            —Adrienne Rich, "Heroines"

When you see a guy in a room
you think is extraordinary,
and you are strongly aware of his presence,
and you think of wanting not a walk with him,
or a good conversation, but to fuck him,
when you're wondering about his body
and feeling it in yours,
trust that.

You know the woman
who fixes her eye on some beautiful man
and determines he will be hers
only because she's hot,
because she wants it,
only because he turns her on.
Be like her.

She is the marked woman who listens to her body
and trusts it
and risks everything for love.
She makes her mistakes bravely.
She shows you how to live.

She has left the church
because their god is spirit,
because they say she's supposed to be like him,
to pretend she doesn't have a body.
They say if she feels in her body
something move, or something warm, or something wet
she's got to shut it down fast
because she's got to keep trying
to be like God with no body.
She has left the church for a temple of trees.

This isn't just about who to sleep with.
It's about clear-cutting old growth in Oregon,
the way they're shaving out huge patches,
leaving the mountains bald.
It's about chopping down rain forests,
parched tongues, dust in the throat,
nothing green, nothing moist.
She says there's a better way.
Pay attention to your body,
she says. *When it moves,*
move.

THE STORM

Being a woman hasn't come naturally.
I have wanted to be a fox, or a wolf,
any animal whose eyes are clear and keen,
who knows what to do, and when.

A storm came this morning at the quarry
after my swim, and I wanted to stay
because the ground was warm where I had warmed it,
and fitted me. I could curl my body
into the round dust nest I'd made
with the bones of my hips.

I thought, *I will stay through.*
I will see the beginning, the middle, the end.
I will be brave, learn how to be at home here,
safe as the beaver in its lodge,
the heron in its mighty, woody nest.

But the seams of the sky ripped apart
and orange lightning lashed
like the tongues of mythic snakes.
In my language, I prayed,
sang the first hymn I could remember,
then screamed into the vacuum of wind,
rain, thunder, *Jesus, let me live!*

2.

When wild geese fly overhead
I always count them.
I know they mate for life;
an even number satisfies my need for symmetry.

Two years ago I saw a duck killed on the highway,
his mate running wild from the dead body
to the road's edge, back and forth,
hysterical in smears of headlights
to the ruined wings, the severed neck.
They may have needed to cross the road
on their way home.
Now, she did not know how she would sleep,
or where. She did not believe,
save for the stinging smell of blood,
any of this could be real.

They feel fear, this is not mine only.
It was as if I saw, in her eyes,
a woman's grief.
It isn't grief, or the fear of grief,
that makes me wish for feather or fur.
It is the fear of flesh,
and finding my mother tongue
insufficient to translate
my wanting to warm myself against human skin
into a language I understand.

3.

If I insist on houses, rooms, hallways, doors,
there is a price to pay.
I have to steal from one place to furnish the other.
This might be called a crime of passion.
So why this panic at finding no den or nest?
I have prepared myself with a language
written in straight lines
like roads leading to a lover,
the gray floorboards of his front porch.
Not the language of leaves, air, skies about to crack.
I have come here unprepared with all my expectations.
Can I leave with no idea what I really want?

Here's what I could do.
I could run the path the mile to my car.
I could drive straight to him,
to where I'd find him watching the storm
from his place on the porch,
doing what people do, knowing how.
I could curl into his body and shiver myself dry.
I could say it had been magnificent.
I could say I failed.

4.

If you talk long enough about what you don't know,
eventually you know you don't know
what it is you're talking about at all.
This is the place hot with birth.

I talk a long time about all I do not know,
the single sharp pain of a pod
broken by the heat of the sun,
the wetness of water, an underground spring.

I am a woman with children, so I tell you this:
When the baby finally slips from your body,
make them lay it against your belly and breasts.
Do not let them cut the cord until pulsations cease.
Press your palms gently, firmly
to its trembling wet flesh.
Go into ecstasy.
Feel the veins throb blue in your sex.
Do not let them take it away
to bathe it or wrap it,
to take its temperature
or prick it with needles.
Keep it there in its blood and ooze.
Know only the anguish of desire.
Let it find the brown of your nipple.
Let it suck hard. Until you bleed, perhaps.

5.

Look. It's dangerous to sit in inches of water
when lightning touches down everywhere around you.
Go, then. Carry the graceless defeat.
Tell him, because you must tell,
it was magnificent.
Tell him you have failed.
Let him hold you.
Let yourself be held this way.
But make no promises, no oaths.
Dream of the day you will go back,
the day you will stay through.
Hang your clothes on branches
to dry in the breeze
at the quarry.
Swim on your back, facing the sun.

BENEATH VISHNU TEMPLE

So We must meet apart—
You there—I—here—
With just the Door ajar
That Oceans are—and Prayer—
And that White Sustenance—
Despair—
        —Emily Dickinson, 640 (1862)

This time I'm alone against the red earth,
scraping soft, brushing away dust
grain by grain, sorting through this shoe box
to get to the parts of your letters
where you have written my name,
where you say *sunlight in your hair,*
that place on your back,
where you say *forever.*
I touch words to my lips,
chips of ancient urns that once held water,
bloodstained shards of arrows
from a time when killing
meant a feast, and dancing tonight,
and food for the long winter.
I date each piece: Precambrian, Paleozoic,
Cenozoic, the Bright Angel Shale,
Hermit Shale, Zoraster Granite.
The winds have cut me, love. Changed me.
Your long-ago rising has petrified
into my longing, and I'm here on my knees
working you into my poem,
so when it gets too dark to write
I can crawl into my blue tent,
my narrow down sleeping bag,
and crystal splinters will light my thighs.
The rest, the cut away, washed away,
blown away particles, will then
constellate politely, and twinkle all night.

COMMUNITY

There are no screens on the windows
at Will's house.
The doors are kept wide open.
Everything here belongs here,
the weather is perfect.
It's May 10th, 6 P.M.,
very green grass, dandelions, lilacs,
acres of field behind the barn.
The sun is settling down,
there are two frisbees flying.

Johanna's making carrot soup,
Gary's brought the wine.
Hope walks around looking beautiful
in her long tan skirt, white shirt,
bare shoulders, dark green hat.
Hal brings bread, still warm.
Kirsten slices a pineapple,
Bob watches her and loves her while she does it.
The soup: Almonds, nutmeg, cinnamon, thyme,
carrots sliced in halfmoons
(*Moosewood,* page 28).

I set the fire, and later I light it.
I am here for tonight and tomorrow.
I have never felt this lonely.
I want the friends who come,
the bracelets at their wrists and ankles,
the curls in their hair.
I am lonely wanting these pottery soup bowls
most of all, the way they fit the curve of my hand,
this carrot soup Johanna has made.

I want never to leave, never to be alone,
some one of these people to stay with me,
to make the same love with me beneath stars
as the one who does tonight.
I want their hands and eyes,
their songs and their stories.
Tim. Amie. All of these people.

I feel myself move among them
as if I were part of this sharing
of cooking and eating and singing and talk,
this washing of dishes.
I want to hold these bowls, to touch
my hands to the slate of the kitchen table,
the counter, my feet flat against the wood floor,
the stones by the door.

In the morning, there is cooking again,
music, contented voices, heavy silverware jangling,
someone flipping pancakes in a cast iron pan.
My bare feet know the warm and cold places
of these floors, and where the prickers are
in the grass on the way to the compost pile,
as if I were not alone.

Hal is carrying pancakes and potatoes
on china platters to the backyard
where a blanket has been spread.
I am a writer and a mother and a woman who,
most nights, is glad to sleep alone.
I clutch my pen like the bone of a child's hand.
When will it fatten?
When can I eat?

HANDS

My fingers are blunt,
knotted at the knuckles,
wrinkled at the joints
like odd configurations of bark
on adolescent beech trees.
My nails look like geranium petals
when they should be shaped like almonds.
Nothing is pretty about my hands.

When I'm at the table, in the car,
anywhere someone might see them,
I hide my hands,
curling my fingers into my palms,
wishing they could shrivel back,
disappear into the sleeves of my sweater.

Am I suspicious of the work they do,
afraid of the things they hold
but do not admit? *Hands,*

you are not wooden puppets
that come to life in the night when I sleep,
you will not creep across the covers
and up to my throat
like props in some horror movie.

Hands, you have held newborn babies
wet and velvet from my womb,
you have scooped the earth
to bury a great blue heron,
you have handled clotheslines
and kitchen knives
and razors in the bathroom
lightly.

When I was five,
I pressed my hand wide open into clay.
I waited for the kiln to make my handprint solid.
I painted it bright red.
My teacher shellacked it, high gloss.
I wrapped it in white paper and red ribbon.

It's been two decades buried
in a trunk in my mother's attic.
I want now to unearth it,
this relic of what I have lost.
Nothing complicated, like civilization.
A simple thing. Something I could hold.
Something I could think was pretty and glad.
Something easy to love.

If I could just be brave,
I would read the lines of my hands
like the maps I love,
searching out the greenest places,
the mountain ranges,
the rivers,
the roads going west.

WRITING POEMS

Because she is a poet,
Suzannah asks her first-grade students
to write poems today.
They look up at her, confused.
But we don't know how to write!
We don't know how to spell.
We can't make words. Didn't you know that?

Suzannah tells them these things don't matter;
they believe her because she is the teacher.
And so, they begin their glyphic poems.
Then Suzannah lets them talk among themselves
about what they have written,
and lets them ask and answer their own questions.

One tiny girl says her poem is about
the man who tied her ankles and wrists together
and made her stand, bent head to toes
for a very long time, *like this,*
and how her mother couldn't help her
because she was tied up too in the other room
and how *he is in jail now*
but soon he will be out
and he will be coming.

He kicked me here with his big boot
because I didn't mow the lawn right,
a little girl explains her poem,
holding her chest.
I didn't tell, but he said I told
and that's why they came to the door
and now he might go to jail,
and I was asleep when he woke me up
and hit me hard and slapped my skin
like this and my mother says she could
make him go to jail but it wouldn't help him
because he has a problem.

Suzannah and I talk over dinner.
These poor little children
who will grow up to hurt their children.
We wonder what chains may be broken,
what new chains we have begun.
Then we sit for a while and say nothing.
Later, we write our own poems,
although we cannot spell, we cannot make words,
we don't know how to write.

DIRTY SOCKS, 11:30 P.M.

Because I am alone
and raising children,
I'm standing in the kitchen
sniffing my daughter's socks
trying to decide whether to
wash them and then use all that
electricity for the drier
so they'll be dry in the morning,
or whether to let her wear
dirty socks a second day.

This matters because it isn't
ecological to run the drier
for a pair of little socks,
but it certainly is not good
to let one's kindergartner
wear socks a second day
when they're dirty
and smelly.
You're not like this.
Your children have lots of socks
in their drawers that they like to wear.

My daughter has lots of socks
in her drawer, but she only likes
to wear certain ones.
I'm confused by all of this.
I haven't said divorce is worse than death.
I've only said my daughter, now,
for the first time in her life,
is having a terrible time finding
just the right socks.
Sometimes she cries over this.
Sometimes she will not let me hold her.
Sometimes she's frantic about her socks
and I sit on the edge of her bed
wanting fiercely to hold her,
and she will not let me.

THROUGH ALL THIS

My daughter wants to know
if it's okay to cry out loud.
I've watched her practice
biting her teeth together
to keep the sounds from coming out.
They're so embarrassing,
now that she's in kindergarten.

Yes, I tell her. *Cry loudly.*
Let's practice.
Sitting together on my bed,
I show her how I cry with lots of noise.
She laughs and says do it again,
and I do it again,
more pitifully than before.
Her laughing is jubilant.
It's okay to cry out loud, I tell her.
I do it all the time, I tell her.

The next morning
she says she thinks she's going to cry
when I leave her at her baby-sitter's.
She doesn't want to eat the carrots
I've packed in her little lunch,
and today I tell her that, too, is okay.
But when it comes time for me to leave,
she doesn't make noise.
She does that quiet thing she's learned to do
now that she's big.

TRANSLATIONS

[She] becomes her enemy
and will in her own time
light her own way to sorrow

ignorant of the fact that this way of grief
is shared, unnecessary
and political.
                    —Adrienne Rich, "Translations"

I wanted to send you this poem because it speaks in threes;
    that year you loved and I did not. I always knew it was
    political, this tear between us. I always knew we loved,
    but dared not extend warm hands to cold and boney. I would
    not feed this demon, ours. Even when the open sky, and
    sun-warmed ancient stones, and my bare skin in the autumn
    heat . . . even when the almost quiet night whispered
    write to her, and I did, I could not send it—
    my love to you. I did not.

Now, at last, we are free. It took the winter freeze to
    crystalize chaos into order. Here on the porch swing,
    the longest dark, the coldest moment, we sit wrapped in a
    sleeping bag. I say *I've missed you. I've always loved*
    you. Your hair is spun gold and my fingertips brush it
    from your face. *You are beautiful,* I say, and kiss your
    lips slightly. When we say goodnight, you whisper
    through my hair, through yours, through our touching
    cheeks, *I love you.* I may never kiss you again.
    It doesn't matter. I will always love you.

BECAUSE GRIEF MATTERS

Joys Impregnate, Sorrows Bring Forth
—William Blake, "The Marriage of Heaven and Hell"

When love stops for some reason,
my language makes sense for a while.
I understand all that surrounds this.
I can explain the thread count of cotton sheets,
the warmth of skin, the candle on the table,
the glass of water. Even the sky outside the windows
above the headboard can be explained.

But I cannot explain the midpoint
of what has happened here,
the falling place.
I try animal howlings,
delirious, on my hands and knees,
my forehead pressed to the kitchen floor.
I get familiar with the tiles in the bathroom.
I laugh, take long baths, eat ice cream, cry.
Drink a little coffee, tea, wine.
I sit in the corners of unlikely rooms
rocking like a stunned child.

Grief matters.
It materializes each sound and movement
into sticks laid straight.
A voice says, *Your hair wants cutting.*
I cut it. It's long enough to braid;
my sorrowing, stupefied fingers weave
together the raft that is ferrying me
across the black tongue river
into the very mouth of darkness.
I keep going.

THE GREAT BLUE HERON

CONFESSION

My arms are heavy with the bodies of men and babies,
pushing, pulling. My flight is jagged,
a dizziness presses from behind my eyes.
Forgive me. I know nothing of the heron.

The morning breezes touch the softest places of my body
and I have opened.
The sun smooths across my belly and breasts.
I have opened.

I have wanted spacious skies to lie down in,
the challenge of thermals, the rush of winds.
I have wanted to fly like an eagle or a nighthawk,
I have wanted to be as beautiful as these.

This morning, I walked the sandy path to the lake.
Beneath cold water, I could not breathe or see.
I splashed toward the sun and scared the fish.

At noon in my kitchen, I held sharp knives
to slice bread, chop onions, apples.
I have never really killed anything.

When the sun set,
the brilliance burned my eyes.
I did not look away.

REVELATION

The great blue heron flies straight
and never stops its rowing wings.
With its long neck stretched toward the place it is going,
it gets to that place never looking right or left.
It stands taller than all the other birds in Ohio,
steps into water with pointed toe,
careful not to give away its hunger.
Then it spears fish clean through
and swallows them whole.

CONVERSION

I want to believe in the great blue heron
the way I used to believe in Jesus,
to make its flying body the mystery,
the crucifix that moves from life to death
and back again. I want my feet to move
with the steady rhythm of heron wings,
my spine straight as its neck and legs
outstretched in flight,
my eyes focused on the same narrow aisle.
I want to be as strong.
I want to go in the morning, kill, eat,
then return to the place I came from
to sleep, to wake again.
I believe when the great blue heron flies across my path
it is the harbinger of blessing, the portent of good,
and because it happened last May
once for every wish I had,
I think *I shall not perish;*
I will live, abundantly.

SUPPLICATION

With bare feet I follow the path into the woods
farther than I've been before,
through trillium and marsh marigolds.
I wonder when I'll get there the same moment I realize
I'm there. They are everywhere above me,
the huge balls of sticks
blurring the tops of towering beech trees,
at least fifty nests.
Then I see them, hear their pterodactyl calls.
There are at least fifty great blue herons,
hovering, shoulders hunched.
It's spring. They are tending their young
or standing watch over what goes on below.
They seem so mysterious,
death's underlings.
I could be breathing swamp gas,
I could become dizzy with the primordial air here.
They are attending me like evil nurses,
I am losing consciousness
and without knowing, all in slow motion,
my cheek gently leans down against
and touches the leaves first and then
the earth, the coolness the coolness
against my cheek the soft, oh!
the scent of the soil!
I stroke the earth with my fingertips
and breathe in deeply,
close my eyes, and sleep.

FORGIVENESS

Was it calling to me in my dream?
By instinct only, did I know
the great blue heron is dead?
Just off the edge of the trail,
its blue wing folds over its body,
legs thinner than pencils, the feet of a chicken.
Its head is gone.
Its narrow neck, a finger's width,
ends like the mouth of a bleeding garden hose
or the artery to a human heart.
I do not know what has happened to the head.

I need to retrieve feathers.
This will not be stealing.
I am going to forgive myself.
At last, I am touching my hands to blue.
I unfold the wing and look,
the perfect gleam of a sky in summer ready to rain.
There are smaller feathers skirting the shoulders,
a blood-stain rust color tinging the edges of its wings,
downy places, the small animal body hollowed of life.
I don't wonder why the head is gone.
I don't let myself look beyond the bloody tube.
I think, *Of course there will be blood.*
This is the death of a heron.
But I do not look, and I do not wonder.

Is this sin? Or a gift?
This pull, my body falling into one
with the body of the heron?
Holding my breath, I tug. It moves, scares me,
like touching dead human flesh for the first time.
This is harder than I thought.
I press its wing joint beneath my foot and really pull.
Eight times I do this. Eight long blue-gray feathers.
I lay them straight in a small pile,
then carry the bird by the wing feathers
(I do not lift it in my arms)
to put it in the safest place I have.
Scooping earth in my hands,
I cover it, set sticks across the mound, and breathe.
Carrying feathers, I walk away.
Before I am out, the sky begins to thunder,
and then pour rain.